I'm A Big Kid.
I Sleep In
MY OWN
BED!

My Amazing Toddler
Behavioral Series

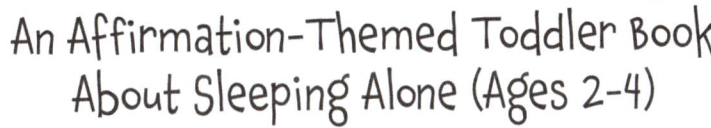

An Affirmation-Themed Toddler Book
About Sleeping Alone (Ages 2-4)

By Suzanne T. Christian

TWORAVENS
B O O K S

Two Little Ravens
CHILDREN'S NON-FICTION BOOKS

Paperback Edition: 9781964202563
Hardcover Edition: 9781964202570
Digital Edition: 9781964202587

Published in the United States by Two Ravens Books LLC, 254 Chapman Rd, Ste 209, Newark DE 19702

'Expand the mind, free the imagination, one title at a time.'
www.tworavensbooks.com

Welcome to

"I'm A Big Kid. I Sleep In My Own Bed!"

This book offers a gentle and uplifting collection of affirmations crafted just for toddlers. As you share these pages, your child will learn to feel confident, and safe about sleeping in their own bed.

Each affirmation is accompanied by cozy illustrations and simple text that reassures and encourages. When you incorporate this book into your regular bedtime routine, you'll discover the power of repetition–an important teaching tool for young children.

Get ready for a journey toward independence, peaceful nights, and a more confident little sleeper!

Suzanne T. Christian

I am a big kid,
and my bed is just
the right size!

When I snuggle with my teddy, I feel safe.

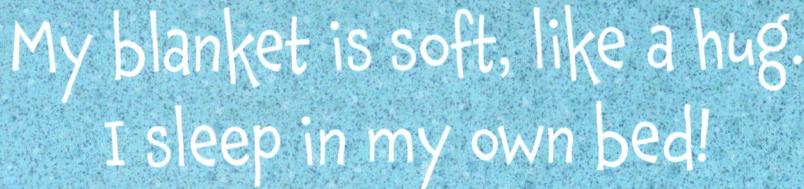

My blanket is soft, like a hug.
I sleep in my own bed!

I can hop into bed
like a funny bunny!

I feel brave when the lights go out.

When I'm tucked in, I feel warm and loved.
I sleep in my own bed!

I have a super cool nightlight that makes my room glow.
I sleep in my own bed!

I can hug my pillow
if I feel a little lonely.
I sleep in my own bed!

Everyone is proud of me for sleeping alone.

I love my bedtime story.
Books make me smile.
I sleep in my own bed!

My stuffed toy friends keep me company all night.

I say "Nighty Night"
to my toys and put
them to bed.

My bed is my cozy boat sailing on clouds to dreamland.

No monster here—just me, brave as can be!

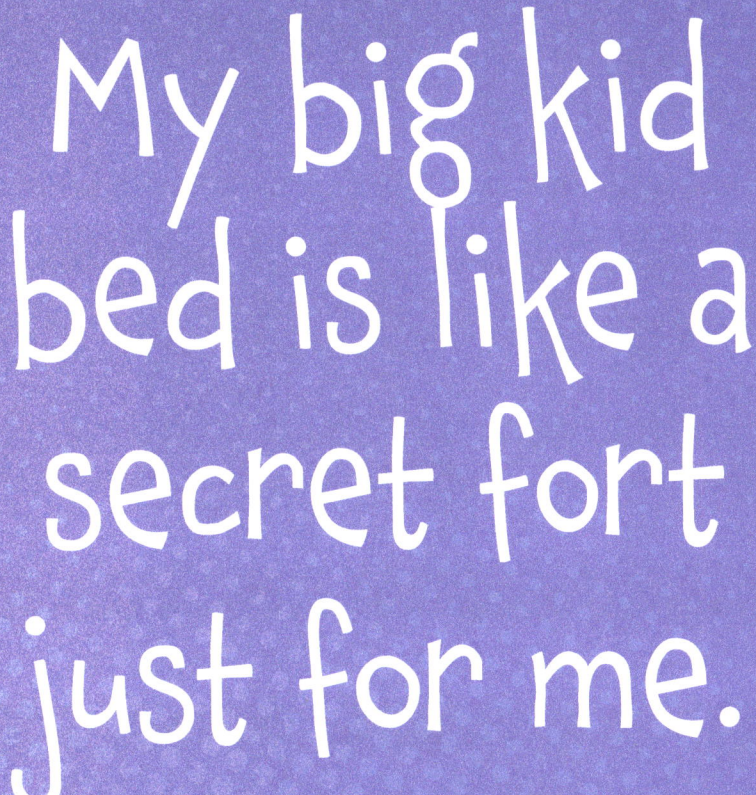

My big kid bed is like a secret fort just for me.

I smile, knowing that tomorrow will be a fun day.

My favorite
teddy and
I have silly
dreams together.

My bed is my safe castle!

Every morning, I wake up and shout,
"Hooray!" I slept in my own bed!

I love being a big kid, and guess what?
I sleep in my own bed!

I'm A Big Kid.
I Sleep In My
OWN BED!
The End!

My Amazing Toddler Behavioral Series

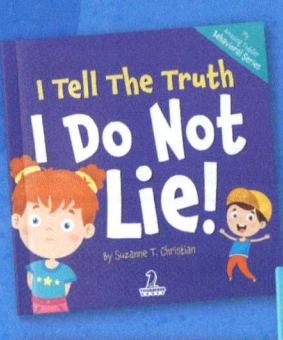

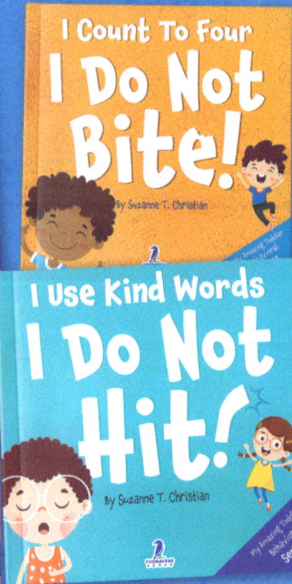

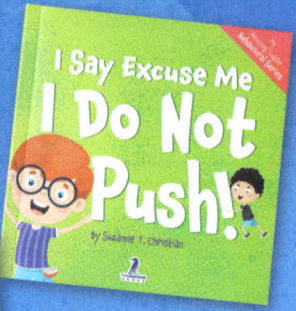

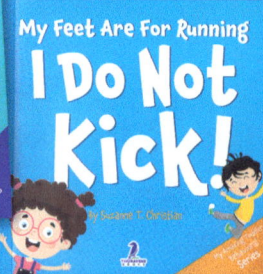

Check Out
Suzanne T. Christian's beloved series
'My Amazing Toddler Behavioral Series'.
Young readers are sure to enjoy!

Two Little Ravens
CHILDREN'S NON-FICTION BOOKS

Dear Amazing Reader,

Thank you for diving into **I'm A Big Kid. I Sleep In My Own Bed!** with me. If this book touched your heart or made a difference for a young reader, I'd be grateful if you could share your thoughts in a review. Your feedback inspires my future work and helps others discover the magic within these pages.

I'd love to hear from you directly if you have suggestions or ideas for improving the book. Please feel free to reach out to me at **suzanne.christian@tworavensbooks.com.** Your voice counts, and I cherish it deeply.

With heartfelt gratitude,

www.ingramcontent.com/pod-product-compliance
Lightning Source LLC
Chambersburg PA
CBHW041438120626
46547CB00002B/259